# Hygge Home

Keep Your Home Life Simple with Danish Living Concepts

Thomas Nielson

Thomas Nielson

Hygge Home

Copyright © 2018

Self-published, Hot Book Publishing

All rights reserved.

No part of this publication may be reproduced, stored in retrieval system, stored in a database and / or published in any form or by any means, electronic, mechanical, photocopying, recording or otherwise, without the prior written permission of the publisher.

Hot Book Publishing

HotBookPublishing.com

michael@HotBookPublishing.com

# Table of Contents

*Introduction* ................................................................. 5

Chapter 1
The Basics of Hygge and the Home ........................................... 1

Chapter 2
Creating a Functional Space and Deciding its Function ............ 7

Chapter 3
Coming to Terms with Objects and Moving Items On ............ 15

Chapter 4
Understanding the Meaning of Items ..................................... 21

Chapter 5
Ease of Access Means Peace of Mind ...................................... 27

Chapter 6
Dealing with Light in the Home and Hygge ........................... 33

Chapter 7
Space in and Around the Home .............................................. 43

Chapter 8
Clutter and the Stress of Life and De-cluttering for Mindfulness .............................................................................. 47

Chapter 9
Organizing Each Room ........................................................... 53

Chapter 10
Bringing the Outside In ........................................................... 59

## Chapter 11
Bringing Peace to the Home via Decorating ...................... 65

## Chapter 12
Useful Tips for Each Room in the Home .......................... 73

## Chapter 13
Summing Things Up ............................................................ 79

# Introduction

Picture this for a moment. Walking in your front door after a hard day at work filled with stress and pressure, you are greeted by a comfortable, relaxing space where you can unwind at your leisure.

Sound idyllic?

Well, the problem is that so many people are unable to do that. They are unable to come home and feel as if they are surrounded by peace and serenity, because they have not created that kind of atmosphere.

That is an absolute crying shame. We should all be able to go home and feel as if it is our own perfect little space. We should have areas where the pressures and stresses of the outside world simply drift away as we cocoon ourselves with peace, serenity, and a calming atmosphere.

But how? Where do you even begin?

Well, that's where this book is going to prove to be useful. This book is all about helping you to create that very atmosphere. It's all about helping you to bring some order to your home, creating space so you can breathe, and incorporating those little hints of comfort and peacefulness that can end up meaning the world to you.

This book is all about *hygge*, the Danish concept of cozy and comfortable living. It's not about materialism or boasting about what you have in life. It's more about the essence of an object and what it can bring to you and your life.

Throughout this book, we will guide you on how to de-clutter and de-stress your home and, as a result, your life as well. We will guide you as to how to remove those objects that no longer mean that much or are taking up space and how to create that comforting setting that you have been dreaming about.

The Danes are voted the happiest nation in the world and when you consider that they come from a country that has harsh winters and hours of darkness, then that's an impressive feat. It's a feat that is known to have been achieved thanks to the concept of hygge. If it's capable of making them happy with their lives and their homes, then surely it's worth exploring.

So, what are we going to do?

Well, there are many different aspects of hygge and how to apply its concepts in your home, so we have a lot to get through. However, there's no pressure being applied as that in itself could be classed as being anti-hygge, and what would be the point in that?

*Coming to Terms with Objects and Moving Items On*

We are going to take you on a journey through your home and help you to apply the rules and concepts of hygge wherever possible. There are going to be some changes that need to be made, but at the end of the day your home will be far more peaceful and serene than ever before.

With hygge, you get out what you put into it, but the one thing we do recommend right from the outset is that you invest your heart and soul from the start. After all, hygge is intended to help those two very things.

Take a deep breath and prepare yourself for something that is going to bring you a sense of calm that you thought you would never be able to achieve.

Chapter 1

# The Basics of Hygge and the Home

Before one begins this delightful journey into 'Hygge' and the home, there has to be some sort of understanding about *hygge* and what it means. Also, one might ask why the world suddenly made an *old traditional* style of living a *buzz word*, something new and exciting, something special and different?

The word hygge is pronounced as 'Hoo oogah,' and while pronunciation is pretty easy to impart to a reader, the actual meaning is a little more complex.

In today's world where everything appears to be busier, faster, and more intricate, hygge's very simplicity has become hard to assimilate or to understand. However, by focusing on the home throughout this book, you will begin to bring together the various aspects of this

Danish approach to the way of living and start to employ them in your own home.

There is no direct translation for hygge, and this is perhaps why it is both special and elusive. Hygge is mostly about comfort, a mindful approach to anything and everything, a certain coziness, an earnest simplicity that warms the hearts of friends and family alike. Surely this is something that you would love to apply to your own home and personal surroundings?

Warmth being key, since hygge is a part of life in most Scandinavian countries and as many people know there is little warmth or light for the majority of the year. Cold, bleak landscapes are touched by the warmth and pleasure of what is primarily a state of mind followed by a set of actions. It's no surprise that the home, and making a home as cozy as possible, is at the absolute root of hygge.

Hygge is not singularly attributed to cold weather; it can be enjoyed in any season. In fact, enjoying the seasons is really part of hygge, too.

In this book, hygge is taken apart gently and placed neatly into our life and into your home.

The home is where we are nurtured, sustained, loved and cared for, no matter our personal situation. We could have a large family, an interestingly diverse family, or we could be living on our own, such is the world today. However, the principles remain the same, and the outcome also remains the same.

Hygge is not prescriptive. It is not judgmental. It is everything you've learned undone and redone. It is a little like going back to basics and to the things that matter to us. It is a beauty that does not cost money, does not entertain debt, and does not pressure people into living a certain way. It is a way of life that nurtures and gently wraps each individual in a life blanket making them feel loved, cared for, and appreciated.

In a world survey, it was discovered that Danish people are one of the most happiest groups of people in the world. This might be hard to get one's mind around, since as mentioned earlier Denmark is clothed for the most part of the year in a semi-dark coat of what could be considered bleakness. It's no surprise that the home then forms an integral part of hygge and that the Danes do their best to make it as comforting as possible.

Let us consider this when reading the above sentence. Add some lanterns, laughter, and friends to this bleak landscape and what do you have? You have a certain kind of magic that can easily be applied to your own personal space. Each element is important because without bleakness, the lanterns could not spill their warm, comforting light upon the gray snow, illuminating it into silver shimmering plateaus. This is the stuff that dreams are made of. This is where happiness resides.

Also, can you just imagine the positive feelings you would have coming home from work and knowing that you will encounter that kind of happiness the moment you walk through your front door?

There is a certain kind of 'letting go' involved in hygge. Letting go of ideas, objects, thoughts and ideation's that do not serve us. It is also a little bit about delving into our very core and understanding what our priorities are, and then creating a life that is worthwhile and happy for us. However, the only way in which you can really hope to achieve this is by starting with your own home. Hygge allows you to create that calm atmosphere where you wake up and feel ready to start the day as you aren't surrounded by that chaos that is common in the world.

In the chapters that follow, the home is the focus of hygge and also the heart. The home as mentioned before is the place where we can begin our journey—a journey of peaceful harmony that will spill out to all other areas of our lives.

We will understand that clutter, useless objects, and materialism are overrated. Find happiness in the smaller, simpler things in life. Happiness and contentment cannot be bought, but they can be learned to an extent.

The home is where we can create ourselves, create our own ideal space, and learn more about ourselves and how to become peaceful in mindfulness. How on earth can you ever hope to do that if you are not in what you determine to be your ideal space? By adopting these Danish methods in each and every room, you can start to create that sense of solace that you have been craving.

By de-cluttering, understanding what a room should really be used for, by allowing easy access to everything you need, and a real sense of organization, you will bring that calmness to your home. Now, how good does that sound? Are you ready to incorporate those ideas into your own life?

Each person's idea of a comfortable, peaceful home is different, and all of this will be taken into account. It is really about putting what you already know deep inside of you into concrete form. It is also a bit about searching within in order to find a new way of living away from the hustle and bustle of life, but more importantly it's about living life your way—the way that makes you happy.

Chapter 2

# Creating a Functional Space and Deciding its Function

Now that you have a better understanding of the basic concepts of hygge and its connection to your home, we can start to take things further to help you in the implementation of the various aspects. By doing so, you will eventually find yourself living in a space that is not only your own but is functional, calming, and serves its purpose, no matter what that may be.

You have to admit, that does sound pretty special.

## Getting Things Started

The first thing for you to do is to consider the space as this plays a central role in hygge. You may think that your home is already all laid out with different ideas for the rooms, but are you actually happy with them? Does it lend to the overall flow of your home? More on that later.

You also need to think about each room on a smaller scale and as an individual. Not sure what we mean? Well, let's explain it a bit better.

Take the living room as an example; you may even be sitting in your own living room as you read this e-book. Look around you and what do you see? How do you see the function of the room? Does it serve every purpose that you think you will need in this room? How does it feel to you? Is it comforting or does it have no real character? Is it lacking soul?

Don't worry; it's not as bad as it sounds at this point.

For most people, a living room will provide a space to entertain guests. There may be a stereo and speakers, a television is pretty much guaranteed, and all of this means that the space has a function. There will also be comfortable chairs for people to relax on and you may have even thought about how the chairs are positioned so that everybody can see one another without any difficulties.

However, are you missing out on anything?

Look at each corner or the space by the fireplace. Are they being used or are they just left abandoned and vacant? If this is the case, then you aren't doing it right, and something needs to be addressed.

This is not to say that each part of a room needs to have its use, but what use is the living room if you have things that are potentially noisy and yet you want some peace and quiet? You have your comfortable chairs in the living room. You can have the warm, snug fire on in the winter keeping you cozy so why would you then have to go elsewhere if you wanted that peaceful setting?

This is where the concept of space and functionality comes into its own. That is where the concept of hygge can effectively come to your rescue.

## Taking the Concept of Functional Space Further

At this point, we will stay in the living room, although the ideas and concepts that we are discussing can easily be applied to different rooms throughout your home.

Stand in the doorway to your living room and look around you. Where are things situated? Can you access everything in the room without too much difficulty? Are there points that you just do not use?

Do you find that as you move around the room, you are constantly banging into things as the place is overcrowded? Does the room bring you any kind of peace or serenity?

There are a number of questions that need to be addressed here, but they are all pertinent if you are serious about adopting hygge into your life and your home. There should be a sense of flow, a feeling of ease as you move around. You should be aware of what the purpose is of any given space at any given time, or even just what it could be turned into in an instant.

Hygge teaches you that there is no point in having that dining table and chairs if it's crushed into a corner never to be used. It gets even worse if the table top is covered in objects and just taking up space. There's no point in having a room that feels as if it is almost going to suffocate you because of the multitude of objects that are contained within it.

But how do you change this? What approach is best for you to take?

Well, the entire idea of this chapter is just to get you thinking about not only each room but each corner of the room along with each object. You need to do this in accordance with the principles of mindfulness as that alone is known to soothe the mind.

## Drawing Up Your Plan of Functionality

With hygge, there is a real sense of you putting some thought into each action and decision that you make in your home. Doing things in a rushed manner without thinking about it is just a sign of the chaotic world that we tend to live in—a world that we are so desperately trying to extract ourselves from.

It's fair to assume that if our home life is chaotic and without function, then the rest of our life is probably the same. There is a need for you to feel connected to the space. That you, and anybody else, is able to identify what the space is for and are free to use it for that purpose.

How can that happen if you have no idea what is actually going on?

Now, we aren't saying that you need to walk around the home like some kind of surveyor and spend an extraordinary length of time studying all of this, but by the same measures, this isn't something to be done in an instant.

You see, a plan of functionality ties in with something that we will be addressing later on, which is organization and space in accordance with the ideas of hygge. However, you need to know the function of a room to then know how to organize it, or else you will just confuse yourself from the outset.

Also, this is not something that you can do on your own. Instead, there has to be a consultation with everyone that will be using the space, or you can easily find one individual not best pleased with a room, and those negative feelings are not in accordance with what you are hoping to achieve.

## The Conclusion Regarding Functionality

It's understandable if you feel that this entire concept of functionality is rather confusing as it can be a difficult idea to get a grip on at first. However, as it plays a central role in the entire idea of hygge in and around the home, then you need to spend time studying it.

To help, these points are the key things to always have at the forefront of your mind, and knowing them may make it easier for you to move forward and apply the rules to your own home.

- Functionality means you know what the room is being used for.
- Consider breaking down the room into smaller areas and their function.
- Remember, a room can have more than one function.
- Have a clear idea of where things will go in a room.
- Once you understand the functionality, you can then start to work on the space.
- Objects are related to the functionality.

*Coming to Terms with Objects and Moving Items On*

As we said, when you are aware of the function of a space, you are then able to move onto the next point, which is starting to deal with your belongings and, once again, this is an important part of hygge.

Chapter 3

# Coming to Terms with Objects and Moving Items On

From the previous chapter, you should have started to gain an idea of the important role that is being played by objects and their function in the entire approach to hygge. In this chapter, we will explore the role of objects even further.

Here, we stress the importance of allowing certain objects to move on and not to feel bad about it. After all, feeling bad about something is not exactly working along with the concept of mindfulness as you enter a dark cycle of sadness, and that is the antithesis of what hygge is all about.

So, let's explore objects in your home and life a bit further and see how you can prepare yourself for potentially letting go. Remember, often the letting go part is the hardest stage, but once you get through it, the sense of freedom that you experience makes it all feel worthwhile.

This is something that can take some time for you to work through, but work through it you must if you do indeed aspire to fully embrace hygge in and around your home. Of course, the length of time it will take is dependent on how large your home is and also how many objects you own, but the concepts stay the same regardless.

## Looking at the Objects

The length of time it will take to go through objects in your home will vary depending on what you own, but the concept remains the same.

In Denmark, it is not generally accepted in society for people to own a number of different items. This extravagance is frowned upon by society, so it's unusual for homes to be as full as they tend to be in other countries. However, they are still going to look at the objects that are in their possession and fully assess their role in the home.

Their normal approach is that you only own what you need. For the Danes, this approach is more important than the price they pay for items.

*Coming to Terms with Objects and Moving Items On*

That being said, what should your approach be with your own objects?

Well, the first thing is to actually take stock of what you have. You need to be aware of the objects you own, as this is the only way in which you can then ever hope to decipher their functionality or purpose and how it fits into your plans for each room.

To do this, you must try and move past the concept of just 'liking' an object because feeling this way is different to it having a purpose.

Think of these questions before you go any further:

- How much do I like it?
- What is its role?
- Does it fit in with the proposed function of the room?
- Is it the only one I have, or do I have more of the same?
- Do I have similar objects elsewhere in the home?

We are talking about some very basic questions, and yet they can make it so much easier for you to come to an understanding of what objects you should perhaps hold onto and those objects that may be best served elsewhere.

However, even when it comes to throwing out objects or moving them on, the Danes don't do it without any thought. We will look at this next.

## Moving Items on in the Correct Manner

Finally, we have to quickly mention the importance of moving the items on in the correct manner. You see, most of us have a tendency to just throw things in the trash once we have finished with them, but is that the correct thing to do?

It's perhaps best to remember the saying 'another man's trash is another man's treasure' because that phrase in itself is hygge. Just because you no longer require it doesn't mean that everybody else will feel the same way.

So, how do you move items on in the correct manner if you aren't just throwing them away? Well, it's all to do with your state of mind at the time and the thoughts that go into the entire process.

You need to understand that there is a very strong concept of sharing in hygge and this is something that all Danes will do, and there's no doubt that it does bring its own sense of happiness. However, most of us will have never thought about doing it with items we own, and this is a shame.

For the Danes, there is a sense of enjoyment in moving items on to a new home, whether it be donating to a charity or giving the object to a friend or relative that has expressed their love or desire for the object. Either of these options brings with it real satisfaction, and then you have the added benefit of knowing that the item is no longer cluttering up your space.

In other words, you are going to win on more than one level.

## Completing the Initial Analysis of Objects in the Home

We will be spending more time looking at objects in different areas throughout this book. However, at this point, our main focus has been on just trying to get you prepared for looking at what you own.

Only a small percentage of people actually do this, and that's one reason why we have this amazing ability to accumulate 'stuff.'

Thanks to their approach, the Danes manage to avoid this particular issue as they are aware of what they are looking for, how it fits in, and the role it plays before they spend money. Also, they understand if they already have something that will fit the bill, which does make life so much easier.

You will also find that they are methodical in how they go about things. They study objects, think about them, discuss them with others if required, and come to a well-considered opinion as to what should happen to it. If the item is to be moved on elsewhere, then they do so with a happy heart and thank the object for the service and pleasure it has given them.

If you pass on an object with a happy heart and have come to terms with the idea that it will then belong to someone else, then there's little chance of you regretting your decision later. That's also why they spend time being aware of their belongings as it then makes the decision to let it go so much easier to make.

So, to complete the analysis of what you have in your home, we recommend doing this:

- Work through the items in each room and be prepared to have a clear out.
- As before, check if you have more than one and, if so, do you need it?
- Consider if an object can be used elsewhere in the home.
- Accept if something has had its time with you.

Allow it to go elsewhere so it can be enjoyed and bring pleasure.

Chapter 4

# Understanding the Meaning of Items

By understanding the actual meaning of items, it allows us to better find their purpose in our lives. Remember, we can all develop various attachments to items that do not actually serve any need, and yet that is often deemed to be enough for us to hold onto them for a ridiculous period of time.

The result is an accumulation of clutter that we have artificially attached ourselves to and that's not exactly going to make life easy for us when it comes to us trying to sort both your home and life out.

Of course, this should never lead to you just throwing objects out because you feel that you have to, just as we covered in the previous chapter. Instead, hygge in this context is all about being at one with the object and truly understanding what it means.

You are never going to throw everything out because you feel that you now need to adopt a minimalist lifestyle. That's not the idea at all.

So, what do you do?

Let's go through some examples.

## Getting Back to Basics with Items

Often, one can have an item that has sentimental value, but where do those sentiments come from, and what is their role in your life? Does the item bring you happiness, or does it weigh you down with the expectation that you should keep it?

As you can imagine, the first part is following the idea of hygge, and being weighed down is very anti-hygge and should be avoided.

Now, this may seem to be a tiring issue to get involved in, but the truth is that working through the basic reasons behind you having an item can actually be rather healing. It can help you to release some inner emotions and feelings and bring a sense of happiness and fulfilment that may have otherwise been missing, and who could ever see that as being a bad thing?

Okay, that all sounds slightly hippy-esque, and it's otherwise been missing, and who could ever see that as being.

Often, we can have items in our possession that have little personal meaning to us. However, we feel obliged to hold onto them for fear of upsetting others. This will tend to lead to our homes being filled with objects that we don't want, and that alone is going to give us some stress.

To deal with this situation, you need to be prepared to spend time thinking carefully about each item and the role that it plays. We mentioned this in brief in the previous chapter, but thanks to the position it holds in the Danish concept of hygge and bringing peace to the home, it's worth talking about it again.

## Looking at Objects More Closely

Here's the problem with items we own at any point in our lives. If we kept everything that we have ever liked, then we would need a mansion just to store everything. Our homes would be crammed full of objects that, to be honest, have no real role other than some kind of sentimental value that may even have been lost to us.

Now, we aren't saying that Danes don't have those sentimental feelings; they do. However, they are more honest in what objects mean to them whereas we tend to be absorbed by those thoughts that go through our mind.

So, how do we recommend that you do this? How do you bring hygge into your home and adopt the methods used by the Danes?

Well, thankfully it's easier than most expect, which should come as a relief to you. For most, the best approach is to actually begin with taking just one room at a time. Of course, you already know what your planned function is for that room, so life is easier.

When looking at your objects in a room, please do consider the following points just to make life that bit easier:

- When did I last use it?
- Is it serving a purpose?
- What difference does it make to my life?
- Does it fit in with the idea I have surrounding the function of the room?

Ascertaining what should be kept, what should be moved or re-purposed, and what should be disposed of is important.

## Considering the Sentimental Value

We mentioned earlier in the chapter that the sentimental value of an object is important, but just how big a role does it play in your life?

It's clear that some people have attachments to objects more than others; we are all different, but you need to really get to the root of these thoughts and feelings before you can go any further.

This also applies to those family heirlooms that we seem to gather. Now, they will often have some kind of meaning, but do you really understand the true meaning? You would be surprised at how these items or those that we have a false sense of attachment to can clutter up our homes. All this does is add more items to a room and detracts us from the true function of the space.

So, what do you do? Well, as we have been doing throughout this book, there are a number of important points to consider and questions to ask yourself that should make this part smoother.

- Does it have genuine sentimental value, or is it forced on you?
- Is there another way you can keep the memory of the item?
- Is it serving a purpose?
- Does it fit in with the function of the room?
- Can it be moved elsewhere?
- What difference does it make to your life?

This isn't about clearing out things for the sake of it; there's more to it than that. However, the thing about hygge and the Danes is that they don't believe in having objects in their home if there's no genuine need for them. This is clutter, even if it means something to somebody else. We will look into clutter in another chapter.

Chapter 5

# Ease of Access Means Peace of Mind

At this stage, we are building up to the point of where we take you through the entire de-cluttering concept, but in this chapter, it's more about the importance of mindfulness in the home and how that has an impact on decisions that you will then make.

However, what do we actually mean by peace of mind, and how does it fit into the concept of 'ease of access?' Admittedly, it does sound as if the two just cannot go together, but that's not the case at all. Instead, the two work in tandem. It's just a matter of knowing how.

Try to think of things from this perspective. A room in your home can also be a passageway to move between spaces. Now, do you want to have to walk around numerous items and step over obstacles to get from A to B?

Absolutely not, and that in itself is hardly going to bring you the peace of mind that you are seeking while adopting the methods of hygge in your life.

## Taking the Concept of Ease of Access Further

Think about the Scandinavian design elements in the home for just one second. They have a tendency for everything to be well laid out and planned to absolute perfection. Each item of furniture has its place, and often they will have more than one function to further increase their usability.

We talk elsewhere in the book about flow, and this goes hand in hand with the point we are discussing now. To help, let's take these ideas out of the home for just a moment and think of a department store. Picture yourself walking in the door to be then faced with a number of counters selling various brand names and products.

Often, there is a flow between them, but more importantly, you can get to all of their items without encountering any problems. How frustrated would you be if displays were blocking what you were trying to get to? How would you react?

The answer is that you would probably react in a negative manner, including getting angry and fed up. Something that should have been pleasurable is no longer pleasurable. It has been replaced by a stressful situation, and that can then have an effect that hangs around in your mind for a considerable period of time.

The very same thing applies to your home.

## Improving the Layout

So, how do you go about actually solving this particular problem?

Well, you have to remember the things we have looked at so far, which means the ability to understand the objects in your home and also the function of the different spaces. Without these two things, you stand no chance of actually being able to work at improving the access in a room, not to mention your overall home.

It's important that these things all work in tandem. Let's look at a room in the home as an example of how this can all come together.

To give some sense of continuity, we will look at the living room once again. Now, as you know, the living room has a number of different functions, and that is where the importance of layout and access comes into play.

Let's say that in your living room you have a stereo system, a television, chairs, and a fireplace. The aim of hygge is that you can use anything and everything in a room without too much effort.

This means you should be able to see the television from each chair without having to move it or change your angle to sit comfortably. Nobody should be sitting in direct line of the fire, so they are far too hot while everyone else is comfortable. Everybody should be capable of switching any devices on without having to lean over other objects. People should be able to get to their seats and feel relaxed. Lights should be able to be switched on and off without too much difficulty.

As you can see, the idea of looking at the layout of a room is that the function is fulfilled without things having to constantly be adjusted. That in itself is stressful and frustrating, and you can start to see how that is against hygge. Also, it makes perfect sense that the more cramped a room is because of clutter, then the harder it is to do all of these tasks without running the risk of knocking things over, having to move things, and just generally being annoyed.

So, when thinking about the ease of access concept, think about these points.

*Ease of Access Means Peace of Mind*

- Can you access each piece of furniture without any difficulty?
- Which objects obstruct you?
- Can you use everything without having to alter the position of something?
- Do you need to remove any object to improve access?
- How comfortable is the room with what is in it at this point?
- Can the function of the room be achieved with the items in that room?

This is all about making life as easy as possible. It's all about lowering your stress and getting rid of those objects that just get in the way. You want to use everything in your home without any difficulty.

Chapter 6

# Dealing with Light in the Home and Hygge

Light is very, very important in hygge. In fact, its role cannot be stressed enough since light can have such an impact on the overall mood of your entire home while also relaxing you and allowing you to unwind.

However, keep this in mind: hygge originated in Denmark which, in winter, has a number of months where there are only a few hours of actual daylight, and this means the Danes have had to turn to alternative options for the sake of light.

Light is capable of bringing a sense of magic to the home. It can illuminate. It can bring comfort. It can completely change the mood and atmosphere of a room or even just a corner. It can also be used to differentiate between spaces that are for different purposes.

In other words, light is more powerful and useful than you may have initially thought.

Once again, we will look at examples to stress what you should be hoping to achieve with light. You want to create that cozy and comfortable atmosphere as much as possible, don't you?

## Light and Leading into the Home

The art of hygge and your home begins from the moment you walk toward your house. How inviting does it look? Is the front dark and, to be frank, scary and intimidating?

Well, if it is, then you are missing the point already.

Walking up to your home should result in your house being well lit making it more appealing to guests. It should have an outdoor light at the front door that is also not too strong, giving it a warm glow. It's the kind of light that makes people feel welcome, while also giving your home the appearance of being alive. That, in itself, is a huge part of this entire process.

Also, as you enter your home, what would be the better option? A dark hallway waiting for you to remove your shoes and coat before you venture forth? Or, you open the front door and are welcomed by a warm space alongside a gentle light that provides a glow and a certain degree of richness?

Clearly, the second one is the most appealing for the majority of people, and you have to think about the way in which it makes you feel about the rest of your home. It should, by all accounts, make it easier to appreciate being home and that you have moved into your own space. It's amazing the difference in feelings that you can have just by using a light at this point.

But let's move into other rooms of the home and look at the way in which light can have a profound impact on the atmosphere.

## Bright Light is Not Always Good

Too often, we have this mistaken belief that everything in our homes should be well lit, resulting in us sitting in a room that resembles the light in a sports stadium. However, the Danes do not entirely agree with this approach, and they have their own opinion of how light works in a home.

The one thing that they do love is natural light flooding in. There will often be light colored furniture, or mainly white, in order to allow the light to bounce off the surfaces and further illuminate the room. Windows can be large and uncluttered to allow the maximum amount of light to shine in for as long as possible.

However, things will often change when it comes to the dark evenings or while entertaining. At that point, light is not seen as being a functional tool to help you to see, but rather a tool to help add a certain ambiance to the room. This is something that the Danes have perfected over the years, and it really is down to a fine art.

To copy their approach, you need to study your lighting in each room. How many lights you need and how strong the wattage of the light bulbs can vary according to the size of the room, but you are going to find out that you actually need less than you initially thought.

## Adopting the Hygge Lighting Methods

To perfect the hygge lighting methods and to then create a wonderful atmosphere in your home, it's important that you begin by turning on the various lights as you would normally do. After this, step back for a moment and observe the room. What do you see?

With this, you need to be able to stand back and actually look at the direction of the light. How much of the space does each light illuminate? Is it harsh or soft? What is the purpose of the light in its current position?

You need to become aware that the Danes will tackle light from a completely different perspective. They don't see it as just being a way to illuminate a room. Instead, it's more about using it in a clever manner to enhance what is already there, and to create a cozy and comfortable atmosphere.

They are still going to have those high wattage bulbs, but they are not the main light source and are merely there if required. They much prefer either lower wattage bulbs, fairy lights, and they are the biggest purchasers or candles in the world, which also tells you something else about their most preferred light source.

Also, a light needs to have a purpose, which is a recurring theme throughout this book, rather than just being stuck in the middle of the room and attempting to light every single corner at the one time.

However, the way in which light is applied to your rooms can be rather specific, so it's best we check that out next.

## Applying it to Your Rooms

The Danish idea is to create special areas in the room due to light and that's easier to do than you may have been expecting. Once again, if we can think of the living room as an example, remembering that the same ideas can indeed be applied throughout the home.

To correctly apply lighting in the living room, you have to stand back and view the room as a whole. Look at the shape of it and where all of the items in the room are positioned. Also, you must think about the purpose of the room as this ties in with the kind of feelings and atmosphere that you will want to create. As light is playing a central role in this, it makes sense to have a firm idea of this before you begin.

The main things that you will be using in this instance are; small lights with lower wattage bulbs, candles of various sizes, and also fairy lights. You might even lights that can stick onto furniture and are powered by batteries. This mixture of lighting can really add something else to the room, so mixing and matching them makes sense.

With the living room, you may have a favorite spot where you sit and read, so for this, hygge would essentially demand that you have a light near that spot that is not too bright, but also not too dim to allow you to do this. You should be able to reach the light in order to switch it on and off when required since the ease of access concept is also very important.

There is also the sense of the correct placement of lights elsewhere. Candles on the fireplace can add a certain sense of warmth and delicacy to the room, as well as providing that cozy feeling that you should be seeking. In addition, adding candles to the top of a table rather than a lamp, or having the ability to switch between the two, can also make a difference. You may also find that placing candles by the window for those dark evenings adds a healthy glow to the room that is both warm and inviting.

It is also an option for you to look at furniture and how it can be softly lit to brighten up those dark corners. Once again, you don't want to just have a lamp as an option as versatility and the ability to change the atmosphere is an important part, so you may wish to consider using lights that are battery powered and draping them over objects in order to bring light to those dark spaces. Doing that in various areas of the room can just add some life without it being overpowering, resulting in the perfect atmosphere.

## Considerations for Other Rooms

Now we will move away from the living room for just a moment and consider the other rooms in the home and how different lighting can be used for various purposes.

The bathroom really should provide you with the opportunity to change the lighting depending on your needs. At times, brighter lights are clearly required for the sake of personal grooming, but even with this, there are ways in which you can alter your approach.

For the Danes, this could involve not using the bright overhead light, but rather having a mirror with lights around it so you can still see what you are doing. They will also try as much as possible to have a bathroom with a window to allow natural light to come in, which is no surprise considering the role it plays in hygge in general, as well as using candles. This will allow you to create a relaxing atmosphere in the bathroom.

The bedroom is another important room where lighting is going to be key. The Danes don't generally believe in using bright lights as the bedroom is a place to rest and be comfortable, and strong lighting doesn't tend to lend itself to that.

With this room, they will usually have small bedside lamps with a low wattage. You might want to take things further and use lamps that have various settings that alter the brightness. This provides you with the opportunity to change the light according to the atmosphere that you wish to create.

Even the kitchen is not exempt from this attempt at lighting and, yet again, there has to be some kind of balance between safety and providing atmosphere.

One thing that Danes do is have a main light as well as other, softer lights in darker corners. They may even apply lights underneath cupboards to shine down on worktops with these being softer in nature but just being enough to add a warm glow to the room.

## The Conclusion on Lighting

The point we are making here is that the Danes believe in the power of light to do more than just allowing you to see in a room when it's dark outside. They believe that it has the ability to really change a room and set the scene, whether the goal is relaxing or entertaining.

What you must do is assess your lighting situation. Throw out the majority of those bright bulbs and lights that dominate, and replace them with light sources that are softer and more pleasant to sit around.

Chapter 7

# Space in and Around the Home

Space in and around the home is yet another central point in hygge. However, modern-day living has made this seem almost like the impossible dream. In the Western world, we often live in smallish homes or apartments, and yet we try to own so many objects that our homes can sometimes resemble a storage unit rather than anything else.

Do yourself a huge favor and take a moment to walk into each room in your home and view it from the doorway. While you do this, look at how many items you have for the room. Do you feel as if the objects are lost in the vastness of the space? If you do, then you are fine, but there's a pretty good chance that this will not be the case for most people.

With this, we cannot forget about the space outside our homes either as we, once again, seem to have this amazing ability to accumulate 'things,' even if it's just for a patio area or a garden. How often do people end up thinking that their garden is disorganized and that they are unable to really enjoy it in the way they should? Once more, we see that this emotion is going against hygge, so we need to consider taking the concepts outdoors to the space that immediately surrounds our home.

## Space is Relaxing

If you look at the typical Danish home, you will notice a lot of space in the various rooms. This often brings with it a sense of calm as no objects appear to be on top of one another, which is always difficult to deal with.

The Danes are content with what the room is laid out for, and they make sure that nothing gets in the way of that function. You should refer back to the idea of ease of access which we discussed in an earlier chapter, as it should all make sense when you think about the use of space.

You see, hygge is about being able to breathe and breathing becomes harder in a confined space. If you are in a room and there's no space, with objects dominating the walls and every surface, then it's not hygge.

It's important that you create a sense of ease in the room. Ease to move around. An ease to use the room in the way you intended it. An ease to come and go as you please. Your home should never be stressful to you in any way, and hygge allows you to work through each room and create the kind of space you want.

## Space is Different for Everyone

Here is something that you cannot forget: space is different for everyone. We all have different ideas of what constitutes space for us, as some individuals feel comfortable with a more closed in feeling than others.

That's why we aren't setting you tasks of what you need to do for the sake of using hygge in your home, as it all rests on your shoulders.

However, we do feel that you should consider several points to help you along.

- Are you sure you understand the function of the space?
- Have you mastered the art of ease of access for those functions?
- Have you worked through the different objects and identified what should be kept?
- How does the atmosphere in the room feel compared to earlier?

The Danes love the idea of freshness in their lives. However, they also enjoy the cozy feeling, and hygge is a balance of both. Space plays a big role in this, and the Danes thoroughly enjoy the freedom that it gives in their home. Identify the space, work with the function you have in mind, and you will see that there is a new lease on life for each room in your home.

Chapter 8

# Clutter and the Stress of Life and De-cluttering for Mindfulness

Clutter causes stress—there, we said it. It also makes us feel swamped with items and puts pressure on us to find some kind of place to store all of the objects that we accumulate through life.

Doing this is easier said than done, and so we find ourselves becoming even more stressed at that thought, and we enter into a downward spiral that resembles a cluttered abyss.

Hygge is anti-clutter.

Hygge hates clutter.

In actual fact, clutter is the complete opposite of hygge, and that's why there is so much of an emphasis on de-cluttering not only your home, but also your life. Because of this, you will feel refreshed and as if you have more space to breathe, which can never be a bad thing at all.

But how does one do it? How do you actually go about de-cluttering in accordance with the relatively rough guidelines as laid out by hygge? Well, the answer to that has to be, "in the least stressful way possible." At the root of this approach is the very idea of mindfulness.

## Understanding Mindfulness for the Home

Mindfulness is all about being in the moment and allowing your mind to focus on the thing you are doing or experiencing at that time. It's about blocking out those external thoughts that allow our mind to race ahead and put our brain under even more stress.

Now, you might be wondering how on earth you are going to apply mindfulness to de-cluttering your home, but mindfulness uses some very basic concepts that are easy to take advantage of.

The first step is to not just start throwing things out; this would be crazy. While de-cluttering, you need to be in the moment. You cannot just get a garbage bag and start throwing things away. That's not what this is about. Instead, you have to refer back to the earlier chapters in this book that looked at objects and how to assess their need, importance, and meaning to you. By doing this, you can then peacefully ascertain if something should be kept or moved on to a new home.

Instead, you need to think about the points we have mentioned in previous chapters.

- What is the function?
- How easy is it to use this item?
- Do I have any attachment to the object?
- Is it obstructing me from using the room as I want?

The one thing that we don't want you to do is have regrets when it comes to de-cluttering your home. You must feel safe in the decisions you have made as to what stays and what goes, and that's why doing it at any time other than when you have a clear head is not acceptable.

## Dealing with that Clutter

Remember the chapter where we spoke about giving items away? If not, then it's recommended that you go back and read it once more because it's important.

Just because an item is clutter in one room, does not have to mean that it is clutter in other rooms. It may be that it is just in the wrong location, so you need to think over the entire house rather than just the room you are dealing with.

That's another reason why you must do this when you are in the correct frame of mind. It's far too easy to make some mistakes, and then how will you feel when you realize this and it's too late to rescue the item in question?

This needs to be done methodically. You need to do one room at a time and understand why you are taking these actions. You must look at one object at a time and come to that decision as to whether or not it stays or goes.

Do a bit of the room, stand back, and see how you feel. Have the feelings that you have for the room improved, or is there still some work that needs to be done? It might take a few attempts for you to reach a point where you are content with the room.

Overall, clutter isn't bad—it's just annoying and weighs you down. Hygge is all about that freedom and only having the items that serve a purpose. Clutter tends to not serve any purpose once you get to a certain point. Do you really need those extra chairs that are never used? Are those ornaments serving a purpose other than gathering dust?

*Clutter and the Stress of Life and De-cluttering for Mindfulness*

Be honest with yourself, as honesty is a good trait to have. If it won't have a negative impact on your life or enjoyment of the room or its purpose, then it could be classed as clutter. However, even after you have managed to throw out the items that you don't need, there's still the organizing to do, which is what we will move onto next.

Chapter 9

# Organizing Each Room

As you may have guessed by now, organization is key. The difficulty is that we often have no idea where to even begin, so we then don't bother at all. This is hardly the correct way to go about it and practitioners of hygge would be horrified at that very idea.

But why do we take that approach? Why is being organized often so difficult or alien to us?

It is just a sign of the general chaos of our lives. We are so used to being surrounded by stress and anxiety that we will often bring it home with us, and that's not exactly helpful. However, there is a way to counteract this, and it involves you understanding how to organize your home and do so in a productive way.

The good news is that hygge sets out to directly tackle this issue. For the Danes, a disorganized room is a major faux pas, and you would be hard pressed to find a home in Denmark that is like that.

Look at it from this perspective. The idea of a home being organized with everything having its place is not just a Danish thing, but a Scandinavian approach in general. Why do you think that Ikea is all about clever storage ideas and straight lines? They are adopting those very same principles where the idea of clutter and things being strewn all over a room is just not allowed to happen.

So, as you would expect, there are a number of advantages associated with organizing a room and it's worthwhile checking them out to really allow this point to hit home.

## The Advantages of Organization

If we can look more closely at what's going on when we organize, we can then begin to understand the various advantages.

First, it de-stresses you when you know where everything is. By knowing that every item has its place, you can find an object easily rather than rummaging around desperately trying to remember where you last put it. This alone fits in perfectly with the concept of hygge as the Danes are all about clever storage and placement of items, so they know where everything is in an instant.

Next, it lets you know what you have. If things aren't organized, then it stands to reason that you could be confused as to what you have and what you don't have. This ties in with the previous chapter regarding de-cluttering your home.

A third reason is that it saves you time. By being able to go to anything you want immediately, it stops you rummaging around and the frustration that always comes with that action. You stay calmer and more at ease with yourself when you know where those car keys are going to be, or your phone, or anything else that springs to mind.

So, how do you do it? How do you go about organizing things in accordance with the concept of hygge? Well, if we are honest, there's nothing special about it, and the vast majority is just going to be common sense on your part.

## An Example of Organization

To really stress the approach that you need to take, we can look at a room in your home as an example. In this instance, we will think about the kitchen as this really does tend to be the heart of the home for most families.

Also, the kitchen can tend to be rather cluttered with things crammed into cupboards haphazardly.

So, this is what you would do if you were adopting the principles of hygge. Now, to make life a bit easier, we are going to assume that you have already done the de-cluttering step and thrown out various items so you are left with those pieces that you really want to keep. So, at this point, you then know exactly what you have to organize.

### Step 1: Understanding Space

The first thing is to understand how much space you have available for storing things. How on earth are you going to be able to sort things out if you have no concept of where items can go or how to deal with it?

Now, this isn't about measuring space or being aware of the size of your cupboards, but you need to gain an understanding of the layout, where the space is, and also the flow of the kitchen before you move forward.

### Step 2: The Flow

The flow is important. The best organization is where items are kept in a logical manner so you can get to them and are not crossing a room or reaching up for one thing and then down low for another. Doing this is stressful and, as you know, stress is something that is frowned upon in hygge.

This is why it's so important that you de-clutter first and immediately prior to trying to organize things. It lets you know the items you have and from that, you can begin to work out the order with the flow in mind.

## Step 3: Grouping Things Together

One thing that the Danes are very good at is making sure that items that are supposed to go together are actually kept together. This just makes so much sense, and you may even be sitting there wondering why on earth it has been mentioned. Surely everyone does this?

Well, you would be surprised to discover that this isn't the case. In fact, most of us are guilty of starting off with things being organized, only for that organization to slide due to us being lazy, not having the time, and a multitude of other reasons.

Let's think of another, simpler example.

In your living room, you probably have a number of different electrical items that come with a remote control of some kind. Now, how do you organize them? How often do you find yourself searching for one of the controls, only to discover that it is in some strange part of the room?

For those that are focused on adopting hygge into their home, they will look at something as simple as the remote control issue and seek to resolve the problem before it can even occur.

With this, they would look at having a remote control holder, one that's large enough to hold every control in the room. The holder would be in a prominent and easily accessible spot and after it had been used, the control would be placed back there, ready for the next time.

You have to admit that this sounds so much easier than controls being scattered to all four corners of the room. You know where each one is and you know where to look when you want to use it. How much easier can it get?

In this instance, you need to look at each room and ascertain which items deserve to go together, whether it be for storage or with how they are going to be used. By doing this, you will then find order in your home, and this will bring those stress levels down.

Chapter 10

# Bringing the Outside In

A huge part of hygge is connected to the concept of bringing the outside in. To better understand this, you can look at Scandinavian interior design ideas and see how the natural elements are loved and adored in pretty much every room. We did, of course, speak about the importance of light in a previous chapter, so in this instance we aren't talking about that, but there's still a lot for us to get through.

In Danish homes, there is often a sense of a general flow between the outdoors and indoors. The two seem to work together seamlessly and this in itself creates a certain sense of calm and order in each room. This is an approach that you are strongly advised to take and we will discuss the benefits of it later in the chapter.

It's no surprise to find out that the Danes love to use natural textures and materials in their home and this has been long known for its ability to relax a room.

## Dealing with Materials

One thing that you will often find in Danish homes is that they use natural textures and wood in their interiors. It seems to bring a certain sense of peace and calm that you have included nature in your home and the beauty that it can offer.

Also, there's never any need for them to overdo these natural materials. The very idea of having a room swathed in wood would be seen as horrific as it can often be rather impersonal if you rely too heavily on it.

What we are talking about here are things that include the following:

- Window blinds can be in natural material.
- Chair coverings can be in a natural material.
- The same can be applied to cushions.
- Other soft furnishings can also be included.

## It's More Than Just Textures

But there's more to it than using natural textures. Instead, by using wood and even including plants placed in strategic locations, you are effectively bringing some life into a room and that, in its own self, is a key part of hygge.

Think of the way in which a vase full of fresh flowers can not only bring a sense of beauty to a room, but also the way that the aroma can fill the air. It brings a sense of freshness not only to the spot where the vase is placed, but the entire room.

In fact, this is a wonderful example of how something so simple can completely change the atmosphere of the room and that's something we have been working on throughout the course of this book. Of course, there is then the need to keep changing the flowers once they are past their best as having something that is either dead or dying is certainly not a pleasurable experience.

At the same time, if you are fortunate enough to have a window that looks out onto some kind of view, even if it is of your garden, then take advantage of it. Avoid cluttering up the window obstructing your view and allow it to become a vista that you can be proud of and enjoy. Being able to look out of the window and take pleasure from what you see is a wonderful thing.

By rights, you should find that your mind is racing as to what you could use in each room, but don't put yourself under pressure to include nature all over the home. Instead, it may be appropriate to have just slight glimpses rather than it being a dominant feature, but this really does vary according to so many other factors.

## Cool Tips to Help with Nature and Hygge

Finally, let's look at some rather cool tips on how you can combine nature and hygge in and around your home. Remember, you can often do all of this on a budget, so drop the idea that it has to cost you a fortune. That is really not the case at all.

### 1. Consider growing plants in the kitchen.

It makes sense to look at growing some herbs indoors in the kitchen. Not only is it useful, but the act of growing the herbs and then using them in your own cooking is hygge encapsulated. Have a corner or a spot next to a window with a lot of natural light and effectively turn it into a small, indoor garden.

### 2. Potted plants in other rooms can help.

Potted plants can be used in more places than you expect. However, one tip is to have something fresh and alive in the hallway, if possible, as it gives a pleasant feeling when you walk into the home. As we said, the bathroom can often be spruced up by some kind of plant in the corner, but it shouldn't be the dominant feature.

## 3. Splashes of nature make a bigger impact.

You want any object or feature to stand out from everything else. Due to this, you need to think about using just splashes of nature rather than it being something that dominates the room. This can be sensory overload, and who wants that?

## 4. Never allow anything to die.

Something that is broken or damaged in some way is not following hygge. So, if flowers or plants are past their best, replace them immediately. Something that is alive and pleasant to look at lifts the spirits at different times, so it makes sense that the opposite would also apply at most times.

Do yourself a favor and look at helping to bring the outside into your home. It is known that being in touch with nature has a calming effect on the mind and soul, so it's perhaps no surprise that it is seen as being a useful tool when it comes to hygge. Also, look at some images of Danish homes and see how they incorporate it into their own particular style as inspiration. However, just add your very own touch rather than doing a carbon copy.

Chapter 11

# Bringing Peace to the Home via Decorating

Once you have removed the clutter and started to introduce the outdoors and nature into your home, we have to offer some guidance on how to decorate your home to then bring more peace to the atmosphere. Remember that peace and serenity are important in hygge and something that should start to weave their magic from the moment you walk through the door.

Now, obviously, every individual will have their own personal tastes when it comes to the décor in their home, but a few general ideas may help to guide you in the right direction. However, do remember that one of the beautiful things about hygge is the way in which you are free to express yourself and do what makes you happy and feel comfortable, so there are no real rules to concern yourself with.

But, how exactly do you bring peace to the home and enjoy a more relaxing atmosphere? Well, it's a lot easier than you may have been fearing.

We aren't really talking about full-on changes here. Instead, subtlety is often the key and it's how you use those little changes that really is important.

We are going to assume that you have already carried out all of those chores about functionality and organizing and that you are ready to add decorative touches that can make a real difference.

## Decorating the Hygge Way

One of the cool things about decorating in this manner is that you can really get involved in the process. Remember, hygge has the habit of incorporating mindfulness and takes advantage of its calming thoughts and this can be extended to decorating.

In Denmark, as well as other Scandinavian countries that include hygge as a way of life, decorating a home is a wonderful thing to do. The family gets involved in the process to make sure that the tastes and interests of everybody that is affected by each room have been taken into account.

There are no limits in what you can do, so why should your imagination be restricted in this manner?

With hygge, you need to immerse yourself in the action of decorating. There is a strong sense of needing to be involved in the thoughts of what each paint color, or flooring option, or window dressing actually means to you.

When decorating, you need to feel that everything is coming together. That you love each item you have used or that your color scheme is exactly what you want. There is no real concept of trying to make do with what you have, that's not hygge. Instead, there has to be a sense of contentment and accomplishment when a room has been decorated. By doing so, you will have a greater sense of comfort in that room.

Also, if you feel that you are too busy to decorate a room on your own and wish to hire a professional, we recommend that you don't do this. Make time even to do one wall or change one thing at a time. Change can be gradual, as hygge and decorating a home is not meant to be rushed. You get no prize for painting an entire room in a matter of hours. In fact, this is something that should be avoided.

## It's Not About the Colors

With decorating, or interior design in general, we are often told what is in vogue at any given time and there is a sense of pressure to adopt those styles or colors in our own home.

Well, if this is something that you do, then stop it immediately.

Hygge, as you must be aware of by now, is all about a sense of freedom. It's about being in your own space, and do you know what comes with that? Choosing the colors or textures that you want to have. To choose the things that bring you pleasure over and above anything else.

If you find that having bright green brings you pleasure, then go for it. Never allow some designer to tell you that it's not in fashion. Who are they to actually tell you this when you personally love it?

If you like that crazy looking sofa, then have it if it brings you a sense of happiness every single time you either look at it or sit on it. After all, that's what this is all about—having a sense of joy in your home. The décor is a huge part of that.

Now, we aren't saying that you cannot look for inspiration. In fact, this is a wonderful way to find out what actually makes you happy as you could be surprised at the answers you get.

The main thing is that the Danes will seek that inspiration and then put their own style or twist to it so that it becomes their own. They don't just look in a magazine or on the Internet and copy what they see. That would only be done in exceptional circumstances where everything was the exact same, but what are the chances of that happening?

## Remember the Small Things

Okay, so painting the walls or changing the flooring in some way are huge decorating jobs, but the small changes can often bring you the most pleasure, and yet they tend to be overlooked.

Take that small table that sits there and looking out of place. With this, you have a choice to make. You can donate it, or there's also the opportunity to re-purpose it and give the table a new lease on life.

For this, you would need to take the rest of what you were doing in the room into consideration, as that determines the colors or the end look. Of course, you can do this with just about anything, so do see this as a possibility rather than just assuming that an item cannot fit into a room because the walls are now a different shade.

In addition, you need to keep in mind those small changes and finishing touches that can make a real difference to the way in which you view the room. Those beautiful lamps that give off the perfect glow. That comfortable chair positioned near the fireplace with a reading lamp nearby. The luxurious rug in the middle of the floor that feels so snug when you put your bare feet on it.

This all adds up, but you need to keep in the forefront of your mind that practicality, warmth, and a use for the room will always be key. Also, stop adding clutter to the room as you have worked hard to get rid of it. By all means decorate with a few small pieces, but never overdo it or you run the very real risk of destroying all of the hard work you have carried out.

This is what we recommend that you do when you are looking at trying to replicate that amazing hygge atmosphere.

- Never rush into decorating; take your time with your decisions.
- Choose colors or materials that you like, no matter what they are.
- Become immersed in the decorating process at all times.
- Create your own style, although do look for inspiration elsewhere.

- Remember the reason for the space and how the décor can reflect that reason.

As you can see, there's nothing too complex here, and yet, it's amazing how often people will make a mess of things when it comes to decorating their home. In the end, you want each room to have its own character and that it fits in with what the room is used for. Purpose is everything and the decorating aspect is not immune to that.

Chapter 12

# Useful Tips for Each Room in the Home

Understandably, we have covered a lot throughout the book up until this point, but it may still be the case that you are sitting there wondering where you even begin with each room in your home.

It's impossible to offer a completely fool-proof guide for what you should do in each room because we simply have no idea how many rooms you have, what the light situation is like, what limitations you have, and so on.

Keeping that in mind, there are still a number of tips that you may find useful when they are applied to each room. Clearly, if you do not have something that is described, then you may be tempted to skip on by, but that would be a shame. After all, there may be tips in those sections that appeal to you and could be used elsewhere in your home.

## The Entrance Hallway

Often, we clutter the entrance hallway with shoes and coats hanging on the wall, but we aren't telling you to put everything away so that the hallway is empty of them.

Instead, choose just one main coat for the season and have that hanging. Cut back on the number of shoes that are sitting there and have a nice shoe rack so they are organized and in their place. Another great touch, which is really Danish, is to have a basket with gloves for you going out, or warm and thick socks for when you come home. It's a little, comforting item that can have such a positive effect on your mind and soul.

Make sure the lighting in the hallway is warm and welcoming, as well. It makes your home look more inviting.

## The Living Room

The living room will tend to be one of the most widely used rooms in the home, so it's important that you understand how to dress it correctly when trying to incorporate hygge into your life.

Begin by throwing out those powerful lights and swap them for a lower wattage bulb. Add some warmth with throws, thick rugs, comfortable cushions, and various candle holders dotted around the room. Identify dark areas and use small lights or even fairy lights to add some warmth to them.

Make sure each item in the lounge has some kind of purpose. Have chairs as comfortable as possible. Allow light to enter the room via the window. Allow air to circulate to create a freshness in the room. Consider using white furniture or throw blankets to allow the light to bounce off the surfaces and make everything seem even brighter than before.

## The Kitchen

With hygge, there is no doubt that the kitchen is indeed the heart of the home. If you have a dining space included here, then you are onto a real winner.

Once again, you need to allow as much light into the room as possible. Also, keep fresh fruit and vegetables on view since this is effectively bringing some form of life to the kitchen. Include wooden chopping boards and wooden worktops with light cupboards. Have a number of cupboards with glass fronts allowing you to add lights to the inside since this adds a different atmosphere to the room. Use small lights underneath cupboards to light the worktop rather than have the room dominated by one single large ceiling light.

If you do have a dining table here, then make sure it is always ready to welcome any guests that may pop in for a chat. It needs to be accessible, take minutes to set, and it should not be crammed into a corner. There should be a sense of freedom surrounding it so that individuals would want to sit there for what would feel like hours chatting, eating, and generally having fun together.

## The Bathroom

The bathroom is clearly a functional space, but that doesn't mean you need to forget the décor and taking advantage of hygge. It's certainly a case of you being able to adapt the room for whatever kind of atmosphere you are seeking at the time. After all, a bathroom should be capable of becoming a space where you are able to pamper yourself, so there's a need for your décor to allow you to switch lights.

With this, we aren't just talking about candlelight, either. Try lights surrounding the main bathroom mirror that will illuminate the room without taking over. Consider plants in the room, if possible, and to have fresh towels. Make sure that there is a towel heating radiator so that you can enjoy that feeling of the warm towel after a shower.

If you are a lover of various pampering products, then always check you have adequate storage and can access everything easily. The one thing that you simply cannot do is to have all of those bottles scattered around in a haphazard way. It's messy, it's chaotic, and it's certainly not hygge.

## The Bedroom

This applies no matter if we are talking about the master bedroom or a guest bedroom, as the same principles apply at all times.

The bedroom is a place for rest and reflection, and that is something that hygge and the Danes are experts at doing in their own home. Too often, people will have television sets, their smartphones, laptops, and various other electrical gadgets that effectively take you away from the main idea behind the room even existing in the first place.

It's no surprise to find out that we are talking about the need for mood lighting here, but also perhaps a chair in the corner of the room by the window where you can read or sit back and listen to music in order to relax.

You see, even though we are talking about removing electronic gadgets from the room, we aren't talking about the bedroom becoming solely a place for sleep—far from it. You should be able to turn it into a kind of haven. Once again, natural light should flood in as much as possible and bedding should be of the best quality that you can afford.

Your bedroom should feel luxurious and comfortable at all times. You should be able to feel snug and cozy whenever you go in there. Most importantly, it should clearly be a place to rest and effectively close the door to all of the stresses in the world. Oh, and using mirrors to bounce the natural light around the room is also a very good idea.

The reason for this chapter has been to try and provide you with a sense of the few things that you can do in order to change a room when it comes to the décor. Of course, we do recommend that you also incorporate the other points that have been raised in the earlier chapters, as it's best when this works as a whole.

Chapter 13

# Summing Things Up

This final chapter will summarize the things we learned about hygge and give you a confidence boost for your task of bringing hygge to your home. To be honest, there's not really a right or wrong way to use hygge, since we are all different and what brings us comfort will vary from person to person.

Perhaps the main idea that you need to take from this book is that adopting hygge should be done with a certain air of calmness. Getting frustrated, annoyed, depressed, or anything negative goes directly against the concept of hygge.

Take your time with this. It is a peaceful process that is done at your own leisure with an acceptance that each small change that you make is going to have a profound impact on the serenity that you feel in your home.

The Danes hate clutter. They also hate things not having a purpose or being in the wrong place. As we said earlier, this kind of chaos is often regarded as being representative of your chaotic approach to life, and that's not a good thing. They prefer to walk into their home and to be met with a real sense of things being the way that they should. Nothing is out of place, and the atmosphere and general feeling in the home is relaxing. It allows them to perhaps forget about the stresses and issues that affect the world outside and when they close that door, they can enter into this wonderful world where everything is as it should be.

You have to admit that this sounds like our very own sense of utopia, and perhaps that's what you should be seeking.

Throughout this book, we have been looking at providing you with some ideas that you can perhaps apply, but you will have hopefully noticed that there have been no set rules to abide by. The reason for that is simple: we just wanted to guide you through things rather than instruct you on exactly what to do. This in itself is a good example of hygge, as it's about what makes you happy and relaxed and who else, apart from yourself, can understand what it is that affects you in this way?

So, how would we sum up what you should do in order to give your home that Danish feel and to embrace hygge? Well, for us there are several things that stand out from everything else, and if you can apply your own version of these ideas, then you will create a wonderful space to be enjoyed not only by yourself, but also by anybody who visits.

**1. Understand what you like.**

When we talk about understanding what you like, we really mean for you to come to terms with the kind of things that help you feel peaceful. What de-stresses you in the home? What brings you joy? What irritates and annoys you and should, therefore, be avoided?

There is absolutely no chance of you being able to adopt these Danish principles if you have no concept of what it is that makes you tick. Failure to do this means you are going to fail in your entire approach.

**2. Understand what you own.**

We spoke extensively about objects as it is those items that we own that will lead to the biggest problems when trying to adopt these principles of hygge and make your home more peaceful than it is at the current time.

How often do you go through a cupboard and find things that you had completely forgotten about? if you find yourself saying 'oh I forgot all about that,' then you need to ask yourself the question, was it really that important to you? Generally, if you forgot that it existed, then it can't have played a big role in your life.

### 3. Be prepared to throw items out.

We generally have too much clutter and as we have said in earlier chapters, clutter brings stress. Also, clutter makes it harder for anything to have order and, according to hygge and the Danes, having order is of the utmost importance.

To be honest, you must be ready to be quite brutal when going through your objects, but at the same time, there's a need for you to work through your belongings with a clear mind and with an end goal to aim for.

Furthermore, it was mentioned that you need to let objects go with a happy heart. You should be content to look at them and realize that they have served their purpose and it's now the correct time for them to be enjoyed by others. That's why donating them either to someone you know or to a charity shop is such a fulfilling thing to do and it is strongly encouraged.

### 4. Be aware of your space.

Space is important in hygge and Danish homes. We aren't even talking about there being a need to live in a home with vast rooms. Instead, as the Danes are not big on being outlandish, they tend to live in relatively modest homes, and yet they can make the space on the inside appear much bigger than it really is.

This is all about making the best of what you have at your disposal. It's about putting thought into taking advantage of each part of a room, and the space surrounding you always having its purpose.

In fact, we spoke about the need for you to understand the purpose of each spot and for your rooms to often be multi-functional and able to switch their purpose depending on your needs at the time. This can only be done when you have a full awareness of the space itself.

## 5. Keep an eye on your décor.

Décor can really make or break a room and this is especially true when you are looking at using hygge in your home. Now, it's easy enough to go ahead and study the Scandinavian styles as they are pretty well known, but at the end of the day, it's all about what makes you happy and content.

However, we do strongly recommend that you are aware of the need to create that cozy atmosphere whether it's achieved by soft lighting, candles, warm throws, fluffy rugs, or anything else that can create that feeling. It's something that you should do in each room and even leading up to the door to your home, if this is possible, as hygge starts from the moment you approach your home.

### 6. Remember the outside and nature.

Finally, nature and the outdoors are very important in hygge. The Danes love to bring the outside to the inside as it adds freshness to the place and it creates a special connection with the natural world.

We mentioned how you should be looking at natural textures and items in your home as well as plants, but please don't forget the idea of bringing as much natural light as possible into your home, as that will make a huge difference. Avoid cluttering the window or having anything that can obstruct it because the darkness can lead to you feeling more depressed.

Overall, we strongly recommend that you try to have some fun when adding a touch of hygge and the Danish way of life to your home. Anybody can achieve it and you don't even have to spend a fortune in order to do so, and this alone is a huge bonus. Small changes in each room can have a large impact on how you feel in any given space.

This can be a real voyage of discovery for you. It allows you to look at your home from a completely different perspective, one that will bring you a sense of comfort and peace of mind. There is no right, and there is no wrong in hygge. It all depends on your own personal tastes and needs rather than obeying a set of rules that have been laid down by somebody else.

*Summing Things Up*

Look at your home and make a plan. Make that plan to organize, de-clutter, and give your home a purpose. Breathe new life into it and you will then find greater enjoyment than you ever thought possible.

Now, does that not sound like a better approach to your home? Does that not sound like something that you would like to go ahead and do?

You bet it does, so get to it!

I want to say a huge thank you for reading my book.

You should now have the knowledge to be transform your home so it flows and keeps you at peace.

These skills will stick with you for life and if you want, you can help your friends with their homes and show them the magic of Hygge.

Just let me know if you need any further help?

I really value your feedback and would love to know what you think, you can do this by leaving a review.

I read all the reviews myself so that I can continue to provide books that will help people with the at of Hygge.

Thanks for your support!

Printed in Great Britain
by Amazon